COMFORT STEW

COMFORT STEW

⊰ A PLAY ⊱

ANGELA JACKSON

NORTHWESTERN UNIVERSITY PRESS

EVANSTON, ILLINOIS

Northwestern University Press
www.nupress.northwestern.edu

Printed in the United States of America

10 9 8 7 6 5 4 3 2 1

SPECIAL NOTE ON SONGS AND RECORDINGS
For performance of copyrighted songs, arrangements, or recordings mentioned in the play, the permission of the copyright owner(s) must be obtained. Other songs, arrangements, or recordings may be substituted provided permission from the copyright owner(s) of such songs, arrangements, or recordings is obtained; or songs, arrangements, or recordings in the public domain may be substituted.

LIBRARY OF CONGRESS
CATALOGING-IN-PUBLICATION DATA

Names: Jackson, Angela, 1951– author.
Title: Comfort stew : a play / Angela Jackson.
Description: Evanston : Northwestern University Press, 2019.
Identifiers: LCCN 2019024816 | ISBN 9780810141179 (trade paperback) | ISBN 9780810141216 (ebook)
Classification: LCC PS3560.A179 C66 2019 | DDC 812/.54—dc23
LC record available at https://lccn.loc .gov/2019024816

∞ The paper used in this publication meets the minimum requirements of the American National Standard for Information Sciences—Permanence of Paper for Printed Library Materials, ANSI Z39.48-1992.

CONTENTS

PREFACE

SLOW COOKING

I pay attention to the news. And one evening the ten o'clock news ran a story that struck me to my core. The story haunted me. I am not a biological mother, but this story of a missing child spoke to my maternal spirit. I began to see a woman troubled by a missing child not her own and, as I had seen it on the news, a tragic end. As I am a poet, I began to hear a soliloquy, and the emotive rise and fall of a voice in the middle of the night was a story in and of itself. It was sometime between 1980 and 1982.

In April 1983 I enjoyed a two-week residency at the Djerassi Artist Colony in the mountains of Northern California. Nestled in the solitude of nature and the company of other poets, writers, visual artists, and musicians, I began to write the play in earnest, calling it *When the Wind Blows*. Chicago is known as the Windy City, and the play takes place in Chicago.

It was full of long and winding monologues like a night wind. The woman talking would be named Hillary, as this was a name I had never heard a Black woman being called before. (I used a name book, *What to Name the Baby*, in those days.) Her man was then named Theodore and called Ted or Teddy, like Teddy Pendergrass, who was a dream performer among Black women of my age group. The daughter was named Sojourner after Sojourner Truth, because I am a student of Black history who entered Northwestern University when the great Lerone Bennett was teaching there, and I actually studied under the esteemed Sterling Stuckey. The mother would be named Alfreda, an old-fashioned name that had something to do with "light" (also, a fellow OBAC member bore the name Alfreda).

It is important to talk about the Organization of Black American Culture, or OBAC (pronounced *Oh-bah-see*), since I was very active in its Writers' Workshop, succeeding Hoyt W. Fuller as its chairperson in 1976. OBAC's mission is vital to understanding the ethos of the play *Comfort Stew*.

OBAC was officially founded in spring 1967 in Chicago. Its founders included Abdul Alkalimat, a social scientist; Conrad Kent Rivers, a poet; E. Duke McNeil, an attorney; Jeff R. Donaldson, a visual artist; Joseph Robinson, a community organizer; and Hoyt W. Fuller, writer and critic, the editor of *Negro Digest* (later *Black World*) magazine. OBAC was divided into several workshops, most notably the Visual Arts Workshop led by my Northwestern professor and friend Jeff Donaldson, and the Writers' Workshop, led by the inestimable Mr. Fuller, who would become my mentor. The mission of OBAC was the psychic empowerment of Black people through the arts so that Black people, thusly empowered, might seize their destinies in the sociopolitical-economic realm.

The Writers' Workshop was central to my development as a poet and writer. Its mission became my mission: to create a literature authentically reflective of the Black experience, to create a literature for, about, and from that Black experience, to create a literature mindful of Black traditions and Western artistic traditions and to be able to articulate the difference. In addition, I added one of the criteria of the Visual Arts Workshop as they painted *The Wall of Respect*: to display Black heroes and honor them. I found the heroic in everyday Black folks, drylongso. Hillary Robinson Clay was named Robinson after my mother's maiden name and after Jackie Robinson, the heroic trailblazer of baseball. Her married name was Clay as in "feet of"—we are all imperfect. Curious perfection of the human experience.

Alfreda, the wise ancestor, watches over the play of events, urging Hillary on, guiding her. She is on a raised platform where it is clear that Alfreda and Enjoli are separate from ongoing events. They are active in memory.

When I revised *Hillary Clay/When the Wind Blows* and titled it *Comfort Stew*, I renamed Ted the more rigorous, tougher Jacob, or Jake, and his last name Sunnyside, a nod to the necessary optimism we must nurture in our culture. Jake brings optimism to the table, and he brings toughness and consideration. The biblical Jacob, of course, wrestled with an angel all night, as Jake wrestled with Hillary's urgent problem of the missing child, and he wrestles with Hillary's resistannce to loving him.

And why did I retitle *When the Wind Blows/Hillary Clay*? *Comfort Stew* spoke to a central action of the play, making comfort stew in the middle of the night and eating it thereafter. And "comfort stew" is a recipe from an African woman, symbolic of our heritage, our strength. A necessary component of love is comfort. Mothers are known for the comfort they give.

Patrice is a name I pulled out of the air. Patrice should be patrician, royalty, but she is not. And Enjoli is a perfume that disappears into the air. It was a popular scent in the 1980s when the play takes place. It is important to recognize that the play takes place in the 1980s, as events of the play were shocking and rare then. I have been told that the play could take place at any time. This may be so, but the play should not be revised or excised to occur at any time. That would be to remove nuance and texture.

This play has enjoyed three productions at the eta Creative Arts Foundation thus far. It premiered in 1984 as directed by the bold and visionary cofounder of the theater, Abena Joan Brown, as *When the Wind Blows*. At that time it was weighty with monologues and slower moving, rich with solid direction and acting. Yet I was restless with my work.

In the 1990s I was a member of PDI, Playwrights Discovery Initiative. The collective included Black playwrights, directors, and producers from across the country, all gathered to search out the future of Black theater. We searched for archetypes and new ideas. I was re-energized in my endeavors in theater that had begun with *Shango Diaspora: An African-American Myth of Womanhood and Love* in 1980, swiftly followed by *When the Wind Blows* and *Lightfoot: The Crystal Stair*. In the early '80s I worked with master playwright Steve Carter at Victory Gardens Theater toward developing *Lightfoot*.

By 1997, when Abena Joan Brown, executive director of the eta Creative Arts Foundation, asked me if I wanted to work with a dramaturg on *When the Wind Blows*, I leapt at the chance. Paul Carter Harrison, master playwright and director, was ruthless in his editing of the play. He directed me in chiseling away the fat from the work. Dialogue was honed to essence. Paul Carter Harrison directed that exciting production with a curious directorial turn at the end.

In preparation for its return to the stage, I revised *Comfort Stew* from a two-act play with no intermission to a three-act play with an intermission. The 2018 production was produced by Kemati Janice Porter and directed by the award-winning actor-director Cheryl Lynn Bruce. This production was a reimagining of *Comfort Stew*. It made use of puppetry as in experimental theater. This production was unique and left certain members of the audiences with something to puzzle over, but the story and message remained. Cheryl Lynn Bruce's work proved that *Comfort Stew* was an enduring work decades after it was first performed.

Comfort Stew is a work of my early maturity, begun in my early thirties. The seeds of the characters in *Comfort Stew* come from my life. My cousin Mrs. Willie Mae Allen Kyles was a devoted pre-kindergarten teacher. She was an extraordinary teacher, skilled and caring. Jake, like my cousin Charles Jackson, was a policeman; unlike Charles, Jake is a detective. The excellent young actor who played Jake in the 2018 production asked me how I created such a believable, good brother. I have brothers and uncles and cousins and friends. Alfreda has the wisdom and tenderness of my own mother, Angeline Virginia Robinson Jackson. And there was a Mr. George Jackson as there was a Mr. Robinson mentioned in the play. Sojourner is the sum of my sisters, charm and intensity, dramatic. Each of these characters in *Comfort Stew* offered themselves up to me—a stew of variety and vitality. Enjoli is every sweet, smart little Black girl. And Patrice is every lost one. This work is dedicated to each of them and more. And it is dedicated to the Erics because I have known one or two and we pray for their redemption. I can still hear the voices of the old women of the Landmark Choir of St. Charles Lwanga Church singing "There's a sweet, sweet spirit in this place." The enduring, powerful spirit of Love and Faith. If you had ever heard them, you would know what I know and believe as I believe: We will prevail.

I look forward to future productions, faithful to the text and vision of *Comfort Stew*. I look forward to telling stories of the people, Black people. The strange thing is, when I am authentic in my truth of my people, Black people and other folk find their truth in it as well.

Thanks and Praise.
Angela Jackson
2019

PRODUCTION HISTORY

Comfort Stew premiered on November 8, 1984, at the eta Creative Arts Foundation in Chicago under the title *When the Wind Blows*, directed by Abena Joan Brown. There was a four-person vocal and instrumental ensemble led by Eli Hoe Nai. Hillary Robinson Clay was played by Martrice Edge; her boyfriend was played by Art Monroe; and Patrice Rodgers was played by Cynthia Maddox.

In 1997, the eta Creative Arts Foundation produced *Comfort Stew* again. The producer was Abena Joan Brown, and the artistic director was Runako Jahi. The show was directed by Paul Carter Harrison, with technical direction by Darryl Goodman Sr. The stage manager was Melody Ross, with set design by Dorian Sylvain and costume design by Michael A. Stein. The cast was as follows.

> Hillary Robinson Clay. . . . . Maia
> Alfreda Robinson/Enjoli Rodgers . . . . Janet Moore
> Sojourner Clay. . . . . Makeba Ayo Pace
> Jake (Jacob) Sunnyside. . . . . Donn Carl Harper
> Patrice Rodgers. . . . . Shasta Phillips
> Understudies: Camille Anderson and Anthony Brady

The eta Creative Arts Foundation mounted a revised production of *Comfort Stew*, opening on April 20, 2018, this time with producing artistic director Kemati Porter. The production was under the direction and scenic design of Cheryl Lynn Bruce, with lighting design by Edward Richardson, costume design by Kemati Porter, and sound design by Sonita L. Surratt. The stage manager on the production was Walker Lee. The cast was as follows.

> Hillary Robinson Clay. . . . . .Raina Lynn
> Alfreda Robinson/Enjoli Rodgers . . . . .Tanikia Carpenter

COMFORT STEW

CHARACTERS

Hillary Robinson Clay. A Blackwoman who appears to be in her mid-thirties; is actually a bit older. Dry wit, self-reliance, and gentleness.

Alfreda Robinson. A Blackwoman who appears to be in her early forties. She is a spirit, quick and wise. She also plays the part of the little girl, Enjoli.

Sojourner Clay. A Blackgirl-woman. Nineteen years old and two or three years younger, depending on the scene. She is charm and intensity.

Jake (Jacob) Sunnyside. A Blackman in his early forties. A storyteller. A loyal, tender, smart man with a restless edge. A cop. A good cop. Tall, lean, and ruggedly handsome.

Patrice Rodgers. A Blackgirl-woman. Lost. Same age as Sojourner. She is thin and keen.

TIME

The early 1980s.

PLACE

Hillary's big kitchen and Memory Space. A place large enough for memory to take place as well as present events. The Memory Space is a platform in three parts behind the now-real space. In the real, stage right, there is a window above her kitchen sink. Some greenery is in the window. A large butcher block table in the middle of the kitchen. This is the stove and table. A pot's on the stove. In the real, kitchen has bench, table. Stripped down essences of a warm woman's home. Props are unseen, characters make them real.

ACT ONE

SCENE 1

[*The radio is playing the Chi-Lites' "Have You Seen Her" softly in the background.*]

ALFREDA [*in Memory Space*]: This is what she said one day. [*Changes voice and body language to four-year-old girl.*] Uh uhn, Mrs. Clay. You wuzn never no little girl. And you ain have no little girl.

HILLARY [*in Memory Space*]: I was no bigger than this puppet on my hand inside my mama's belly. And you too.

ALFREDA/ENJOLI: I wuzn in my mama's belly.

HILLARY: You said the stork didn't bring you. Cabbage patch wasn't it.

ALFREDA/ENJOLI: The garbageman brought me.

HILLARY: Who told you that?

ALFREDA/ENJOLI: A man on TV. Hee—hee—hee—hee.

HILLARY: You turn that TV off!

ALFREDA/ENJOLI: Nobody else could come. Hee-hee.

HILLARY: Repeat after me: God Almighty delivered me Himself.

ALFREDA/ENJOLI: God All-the-Mighty delivered me Hisself.

SCENE 2

HILLARY [*to audience as she walks from the Memory Space to the kitchen*]: Have you seen her?

[HILLARY's *voice rises as the dim lights go up. And she walks to center stage. The lights go up as she progresses through her monologue and simulates cooking in stove/table area. She is singing absently.*]

Rock-a-bye-baby in the treetops,
When the wind blows the cradle will rock.
When the bough breaks the cradle will fall,
Down will come baby, cradle and all.

[*She searches the kitchen for what she needs.*]

I can't stand to cook in a kitchen where I don't have what I want. Gets on my last nerve. And I'm on that already. My little girl missing. I don't know what else to do but sing a broken lullabye. And cook up a storm. Wherever she is, let her be sleeping safe.

I'm making African stew. My neighbor Comfort taught this dish to me. She told me the recipe in her Ghanaian accent. "Chop tomatoes, onions, pepper very fine, or grind it down with mortar and pestle, boil it, add okra and fish, then grind the groundnuts." "Ground nuts?" I asked her. "They grow close to the ground." "Peanuts," I said, "you talkin about peanuts . . ." "Groundnuts, Hillary," she said, because she doesn't like me or her husband translating what she says. "You can use peanut butter if you must—Skippy or Peter Pan, Europeanized groundnuts." And

I said, "My daughter can't eat peanuts or peanut butter. Enjoli loves peanut butter. George Washington Carver, a Black American man, devised peanut butter." "The ancestors whispered in his ear," Comfort said.

ALFREDA [*who has been listening to this as if* HILLARY *were speaking directly to her*]: Comfort would have the last word.

HILLARY: I got up this morning with a funny feeling in my stomach. Flitting just past the corner of my eye like a little bird. When I got to the Center all my children came in except for Tony who always has a cold. And little Enjoli. She was absent. Surprised me. She's always there.

PATRICE [*appearing in Memory Space*]: Mrs. Clay. My name is Patrice Rodgers. And this my daughter, Enjoli.

HILLARY: Like the perfume.

PATRICE [*aggressively*]: I like that perfume.

HILLARY: I do too. And I like you, Enjoli . . .

After that she was there every day. Never missed.

ALFREDA: You knew it was somethin wrong when she didn't come today.

HILLARY: Yes, I knew. Deep inside.

ALFREDA: And that's all you know. The rest is fear. Keep a hold to yourself. Fear can run wild. Remember when you were seventeen and I was about your age now.

SCENE 3

[*In the Memory Space,* ALFREDA *and a seventeen-year-old* HILLARY *enter.* ALFREDA *takes off imaginary coat and sets to work in an imag-*

inary kitchen. She goes back and forth between kitchen and living room. The girl stands entranced, with her coat on. She is speechless.]

ALFREDA [*bustling*]: Hank called today for some money for books. His part-time job ain't meetin his expenses. Scholarship just room and board and tuition. This college business is too much. And Beau says his unit is shipping out from San Diego. I'm glad he's off the streets and into uniform. Though I ain't thrilled about uniforms. He doesn't know where he's going either. I guess they going lookin for a war somewhere or lookin to start one. Wanta heat up that Cold War. Sound like a can of Campbell's Soup. Cold War Soup. Got a war right here though. One right here. Negroes on their knees against water hoses and police dogs.

[*Turns on TV. Lets her gaze rest on the girl at last.*]

Take off your coat. Why you standing there with your coat on?

[*She doesn't expect answer. Looks back at imaginary TV.*]

I don't know if I could take somebody hitting me upside my head. [*Slowing down.*] Your father either. He wouldn't want somebody knocking you upside your head. Not even Life. Sometimes he act like he'd fight God over you kids. I know he'd take a lick for you.

[*Her back is to the girl. She folds a dish towel, then folds her hands. Looking directly at girl now.*]

ALFREDA: Especially you, Hillary. Especially you.

[*This prompts the girl to speak in a whisper. She still clutches her coat.*]

HILLARY: Mama, don'ttelldaddy, don'ttelldaddy.

ALFREDA: How else he gonna find out, Hillary? Wait and see?

HILLARY [*beginning to take off her coat*]: I have to tell Tommy first.

ALFREDA: He was there from the conception—of the idea—so to speak.

[*Checks girl for response. Continues musing.*]

Hard for me to see Tommy Clay as anybody's father. If he was in this by himself, he'd give birth to a basketball.

[*A long pause here.*]

Are you going to talk to me?

HILLARY: I'm waiting for you to talk to me, Mama.

ALFREDA [*snippy*]: A little late for consultation.

[HILLARY *flinches visibly.*]

ALFREDA: I'm sorry. I'm not going to whip you with words.

HILLARY: You don't need words, Mama. The way you look at me. All that disappointment in your eyes. All that sadness. I hurt you, Mama. I'm sorry, Mama. I really been a good girl though. I really have.

ALFREDA: When I think of your dreams. And the bed you gonna lie in. I know it's the bed you made. But it's not what—everybody has the right to their one mistake.

HILLARY: Mine's a lulu.

ALFREDA: One mistake. You are a good girl. You just going to be a good mother now.

[*Holds* HILLARY's *face in her hands.*]

HILLARY: I don't want to be anybody's mother. I don't want to be anybody's mother. I don't want to be anybody's mother. I don't want to be anybody's mother, Mama!

ALFREDA: Yes. You do. Just not right now. You are a nurturer, Hillary.

[*Inspects* HILLARY's *hands.*]

These are mother hands. You want to be a mother. It's not the end of the world, though the earth is quaking. It's what you do with the rest of your self that I'm waitin for. Me and your daddy. Those other dreams.

[HILLARY *turns her face to her mother's bosom; shoulders shaking, she weeps.*]

I'm not crying over you, baby. I'm crying with you. I'm here. Mama's here.

[*Slow fade on tableau of mother and daughter.*]

SCENE 4

[HILLARY *walks to another Memory Space where a man,* JAKE, *is seated.*]

HILLARY: The marriage, like a bad party, broke up early. What was my life like? One bad job after another. I was a member of the bus brigade.

JAKE: What's that?

HILLARY: You got a car. It's the mostly girls and women who carry babies on the bus early mornings before rush hour. An army of mostly girl-women lugging baby, diaper bag, purse, and broken promises on the bus.

JAKE: I didn't take mine on the bus. And my ex didn't either. I saw to that. What happened to you and Tommy?

HILLARY: Didn't I tell you?

JAKE: No.

HILLARY: He couldn't find his way home.

JAKE: Lost in the city.

HILLARY: He just couldn't find his way home. Except to change clothes.

JAKE: What about your baby?

HILLARY: He was a better father—and that ain't great—after he left. It was me he didn't want to find. He couldn't get over the fact that I wasn't a basketball.

JAKE: What?

HILLARY: Never mind. Eventually I married me some college.

ALFREDA [in her light]: Ain't you through rememberin yet? Make some more phone calls to the morning and afternoon classes. She's in both of them, isn't she? Somebody may know somethin.

HILLARY [in kitchen on phone]: This is Mrs. Clay from Watoto House. I was wondering if Malik mentioned Enjoli Rodgers, his class-mate. Yes. Since yesterday . . . Okay, thank you.

[Another phone call.]

This is Mrs. Clay. Okay, thank you . . . This is Mrs. Clay. Yes. Watoto House. Yes. Watoto means children. You were right. Okay. Thank you . . . This is Mrs. Clay, one of the directors of Watoto

House. Yes. Enjoli. The perfume. It is a pretty name. She's a pretty little girl. Okay. Thank you.

ALFREDA: Okay. You can remember some more, but not too far back.

SCENE 5

SOJOURNER [*in another Memory Space*]: Mama! Mama!

HILLARY: In the kitchen.

SOJOURNER: Oh! Mama, guess what?

HILLARY: Uh uhn, I'm not guessing. Guessing is too dangerous with you. I could lose anything. Like my new blue blouse.

SOJOURNER: I gave you your blouse back.

HILLARY: In the dirty clothes hamper? You find it there?

SOJOURNER: Okay, Mama. I'll wash your blouse.

HILLARY: Thank you so much.

SOJOURNER: You still haven't guessed.

HILLARY: What?

SOJOURNER: Well, since you asked, I'll tell you. Mama, I'm going to school in the city, instead of going so far away. That way I can be near you. And the university here is just as good as going away across country, spending all that money.

HILLARY [*subdued*]: You're getting a scholarship to go away.

SOJOURNER: I can get one to stay here. Home. And be near you, Mama.

HILLARY: Since when you been so crazy about me?

SOJOURNER: Mama, don't be so mean. You know I have always been your best daughter.

HILLARY: I don't have but one daughter.

SOJOURNER: See what I mean?

HILLARY: Why you so interested in this city? You been achin to go. You been dreamin your dream of languages for a long time. "I want to be the female Paul Robeson and speak seven languages."

SOJOURNER: I'm just changing schools. Not my goals.

HILLARY [*softly, like the voice of conscience*]: Are you sure?

SOJOURNER: I wasn't lying. I'm still going to be a linguist. I'm still going to learn languages. I have three already. English, French, Spanish, and four if you count Black English.

HILLARY: For some reason, you're not being honest with yourself.

SOJOURNER: I am! [*Growing righteous indignation*] Mama. You act like I'm not graduating from high school. And I'm salutatorian too. And working my butt off on a job and on the honor roll all the time. And in the French Club and the Spanish Club and the Black Heritage Club. I do do what I say. I'm staying here and going to school.

HILLARY [*suddenly grasping the truth.*]: I believe it's that fast-talking, gape gap-toothed . . . boy. You better go and study your languages, girl. He tellin lies.

SOJOURNER: Wouldn't make any difference. No matter how many languages I speak, I still can't talk to you!

[*Characters freeze. Quick fade.*]

SCENE 6

[*In Memory Space.*]

ALFREDA: Now. Remember now. The day before yesterday or was it a week ago?

HILLARY [*in Memory Space, braiding hair of imaginary* ENJOLI]: The other children are long gone.

ALFREDA/ENJOLI: They gone home.

HILLARY: You'll be gone home soon.

ALFREDA/ENJOLI: My mama gone pick me up.

HILLARY: And you can show her your pretty hair.

ALFREDA/ENJOLI: My pretty hair. My mama gone like my pretty hair. Eric gone like my pretty hair.

HILLARY: He sure is. Who is Eric?

ALFREDA/ENJOLI: Eric gone be my daddy. He my mama's boyfriend.

HILLARY: Oh, and what does Eric do?

ALFREDA/ENJOLI: Drugs.

HILLARY: No!

ALFREDA/ENJOLI: That's what my grandmama say. My mama say she don't know that. She don't know no sucha thing.

SCENE 7

[*In another Memory Space.*]

ALFREDA: Hillary, I always told you you shoulda told your daughter about her daddy. But you said you wouldn't touch the respect a child must have for its daddy. I still say the truth is the light. I know it's a fact. That's why I blew that tree down into his bedroom window. If she'd known, Sojourner wouldn't have treated you the way she did that day. Go on, conjure it up.

[*Lights up on* HILLARY *and* SOJOURNER. HILLARY *seated, looks up at* SOJOURNER *angrily.*]

HILLARY: Sojourner Truth Clay, you stand there and you have no sympathy for that girl's predicament. I feel for her. Somebody— you could be her baby.

SOJOURNER [*unmoved*]: She did it on purpose. She didn't have to get pregnant. She trying to trap him.

HILLARY: She's caught too. [*Pauses*] He was a full partner. He had his thrill in the bargain.

SOJOURNER: She went after him because she knew he was mine.

HILLARY: Somebody should have told him. That he was yours. Were his eyes closed all the while?

SOJOURNER: You just want him to marry her. And me to go away to school.

HILLARY: I want him to be responsible for his child. And you to go away to school.

SOJOURNER: Mama, I love Mario. Don't you know?

HILLARY: I know. And I know that child's got to work something out with that child carrying another child.

SOJOURNER: You were a child when you had me.

HILLARY: Don't I know the day my childhood ended? What's your birthday, daughter?

SOJOURNER: Oh, you so funny. [*Defiant*] You just don't want me and Mario to be together and we made plans. I'm in love with Mario and I'm gonna stand by him through this. [*Desperate*] Mario says it's probably not his baby no how. He says it coulda been any number of boys' baby. He wasn't the only one.

HILLARY [*on her feet*]: Hold it. Hold it right there. You wanna go to school here to be near me. You might get married. Mario's got a girl pregnant, but it might not be his. This boy is not right.

SOJOURNER: You never liked Mario. You don't like him because he Latino.

HILLARY: Latino? Is that what he told you and I knew his mother when she came up here from Mound Bayou, Mississippi, and his daddy was a slew-footed boy from Pine Bluff, Arkansas. He a Guadalajara–San Juan lie. What he wanna be Latino for? They ain't much better off than us. He just that stupid.

SOJOURNER: Mama, I love Mario. And I'm going to stand by my man!

HILLARY: Oh, you sound like a bad record and you need to play it somewhere else.

[*She sits back down with a quick dismissiveness.*]

SOJOURNER: I'm going with Mario.

HILLARY: Sojourner, I didn't mean . . . Don't . . .

SOJOURNER: I know you didn't, Mama. But, maybe, I should go. We don't do anything but fight.

[*Exit* SOJOURNER.]

HILLARY [*whispering to* SOJOURNER's *vacated space*]: Don't you know why? Don't you know how much I love you and I can see the end of the road with him. Disaster.

[*Enter* SOJOURNER *with imaginary suitcase.*]

HILLARY: That was some fast packing.

SOJOURNER [*talking fast*]: I'm going to stay with Daddy. He said I could.

HILLARY: When was that? Since when has your daddy been into conversation?

SOJOURNER [*Shifting the suitcase in her hands and facing* HILLARY *squarely*]: Mama, I am not you.

HILLARY: Oh, yes . . . you . . . are. I see you and I see me. I see the lift in my eyebrow in yours. I see the round of my behind repeating on you, and the mole between my breasts, between yours. And my birthmark on your thigh. Girl, you can't not be me.

SOJOURNER: All my life I been following other people. Following up behind Grandmama and fetching for Grandaddy, crying for Daddy to pick me up, imitating Paul Robeson and Sojourner Truth because you gave me that name. And I been shadowing you, Mama. I been a good girl.

HILLARY: I know you have. I made sure.

SOJOURNER: No, you didn't. You couldn't make sure. You weren't with me every waking hour. When I was out of your sight.

HILLARY: I got eyes beyond eyes. I know you. I put me in you. You are my daughter. I know you like the back of my hand.

SOJOURNER: But, Mama, I got my own fingerprints.

[*Fade.*]

SCENE 8

[*Lights up on another Memory Space.*]

ALFREDA: Everybody do. Got they own fingerprints. Like this new guy you met a year or thereabouts, Hillary. Didn't you want his fingerprints on you?

HILLARY [*remembering with* JAKE]: I had to use the ladies' room, remember?

JAKE: I remember, Lady.

HILLARY: Yes. Talking to you was easy. You're an easygoing man.

JAKE [*replaying their introduction*]: Jake. Jacob Sunnyside. And you?

HILLARY: Hillary Robinson Clay.

JAKE: I told you my life story as soon as I told you my name. Nam. College. Marriage. Divorce. Counseling. Shoulda had that before marriage. My two kids. Joint custody. Two flat. Mama lives two doors down. Whatever happened to Tommy?

HILLARY: He married again. And left her with three children. He's on his third wife now.

JAKE: That ain't bad.

HILLARY: And twelfth job.

JAKE: At least he got one.

HILLARY: You are sunnyside.

JAKE: Not all the time.

HILLARY [*toasting with an imaginary glass*]: Well, sunnyside up!

SCENE 9

HILLARY [*switching on the light on another Memory Space*] Sojourner, it's you. You're home. What you sitting up here in the dark for, baby?

SOJOURNER [*shrugging and mumbling*]: Iownknow.

HILLARY: You don't know? [*Sits beside girl.*] You don't know? What's wrong? [SOJOURNER *still doesn't answer.*] Whatever it is, I'm happy you're here. I miss you.

SOJOURNER [*breaks down, crying*]: Mama. Mario . . . Mario.

HILLARY: Baby, are you pregnant? Are you going to have a baby? Tell me. Mama will fix it. Do you want that? I want what you want. Tell me. If you decide to keep it . . . you can keep on going to school and I can stay with the baby for a while. I'll help you.

[*The bluntness of her mother's statement shames* SOJOURNER. *She pulls away and moves with her back to* HILLARY. SOJOURNER *is starkly composed.*]

SOJOURNER: Mama, I'm a fool. You were right all along. Mario. Mario got another girl pregnant.

HILLARY: I don't want to be right right now.

SOJOURNER: Can I come home? Tell me I can come home again.

HILLARY: For a little while. But I'm gonna look around and you'll be off to college. You're a young woman now, Ms. Sojourner Truth Clay.

[*Fade on Memory Space.*]

SCENE 10

[*Light on* ALFREDA. *It is the present.*]

The neighbors say she's up cookin in the middle of the night.

The neighbors say her boyfriend, he's a detective—

Can he detect the smell of her stew?

Walkin down the stairs while he goes up.

The neighbors say is he just answerin her call?

Where he been so long?

The neighbors say a good man is just like Jesus.

He may not always come when you want him

But he sho be there when you need him.

JAKE [*after a quick embrace*]: Why didn't you call me before?

HILLARY: I couldn't reach you. I forgot about tonight.

JAKE: Don't worry till you got something to worry about. Do you know how many kids are reported missing everyday?

HILLARY: No, how many?

JAKE: It's a lot more than turn out serious. Don't let your imagination run away with you.

HILLARY: I'm tryin not to.

JAKE: Okay, baby. Let's just stick to the facts.

HILLARY: Fact is, you look about as tired as I feel. How was tonight?

JAKE: All time low. I started off the evening with a funny feeling. Sit down, I'm gonna give you a blow-by-blow to entertain you a while. I told you about my funny feelings. They don't crawl up in my stomach, like yours, or flit by the corner of my eye. Mine sit on my shoulder like something blew by me. My left shoulder. So I kept shrugging my shoulder. Like I'm trying to get this chip off my shoulder. I'm setting up my speakers for the set, shrugging, then I realize what I'm doing. I catch myself. Shrugging. So I know some shit is about to go down.

I look up and here come two white dudes I ain't never seen before. Kinda mangy looking, like they undercover. They were either dope pushers or undercovers.

I kinda glanced around over each of my shoulders looking for who they looking for. This chip on my shoulder is killing me. It has sunk down and spread out all into my collar bone. I'm trying not to twitch my shoulders or anything, cause that looks too guilty, and nervous. I just don't feel like no stuff tonight and . . .

HILLARY: It's aggravating the way they approach you. Like they got a right to the space in front of your face.

JAKE: Well, that's where one of them stood. Right smack dab in my face.

HILLARY: White folks got no sense of social distance.

JAKE: This wasn't no social call. More like a scene from a bad Western. "Gunfight at Okay Disco."

HILLARY: Who drew first?

JAKE: They drew. First and last.

HILLARY: So what they want?

JAKE: Woman, if you quit asking me questions, I'll tell you the story.

HILLARY: You too slow.

JAKE: "You got a pretty good rapport with this gang meat around here," the one in my face says. The other one standing in the background got one hand deep in his coat pocket. Like he feeling his heat. Or his meat. I don't know which one but whatever it is, feels good, cause he droolin. I try not to shrug my shoulders when I answer. I don't wish to appear too nonchalant. They don't take to nonchalant. So I answer respectfully, "I know a lot of these kids. I do teen sets regularly. Not many djs like teen sets. They're unpredictable." "But you predict good, huh?" Mr. Po-Lease mumbles. "I take my chances," I say. "Maybe you predict so good because you help things go your way."

HILLARY: I don't like the sound of this. Is he suggesting what I think he's suggesting?

JAKE: Nothing but. Feigning here and there like he stickin pins in me to see if I flinch. Needlin me, ya understand? Then Mr. Beat Yo Meat or Hold Yo Heat says [JAKE *holds his nose to create sound effect.*] "Sunnyside Jake, don't try this innocent act with us. You spend a great deal of time on these teen-age dances. Perhaps you give them more than loud music and brotherly advice. May be you're the mind behind a lot of the gang activity."

HILLARY: Slander! Sue, Jake.

JAKE: I said, "I beg your pardon." I had to cough because this chip has moved from my shoulder to my throat.

HILLARY: This is crazy! The kids know you by how strict you are. You're a policeman, a better one than those two.

JAKE: And my partner is a policeman and is supposed to be there, but I hadn't seen him since Emancipation. It didn't make no never mind, cause these dudes wasn't into listening. I told them to get out of my face, and the next time they jump up in my chest they better have a search warrant or a warrant for my arrest. They backed off, cause this blood was bout to go crazy. And chips was fallin wherever they could. The undercovers retreated.

HILLARY [*ominously*]: Uh uh. Things goin smooth.

JAKE: This funny feeling is back sitting on my left shoulder again. So I set up the box for some long playing sides to keep the kids out on the dance floor busy for a good long while. And I just go wherever my shoulder tells me to go. To the boys' room. All of a sudden the door fly open and five of the young dudes tumble out of the john on top of each other. Screaming and snarling like scalded cats. This geyser of hot water, hot, steaming water comes pourin out the door behind them. They scrambling tryin to get out the way.

HILLARY: Oh, my God! What . . .?!!

JAKE: Two of them wrestle away from the water. This fool sling this other fool upside the wall then start to slam him upside the head with a pistol.

HILLARY: How'd he get that in there?

JAKE: Search me.

HILLARY: Didn't you search him?

JAKE: When I searched, they were all clean. But lemme finish telling you. I dove in on em. Pulled him off the dude. Well, the boy musta been suffering brain damage; he bleedin from the head and break away from the pistol whipping clown, and then he runs out into the middle of the dance floor.

You shoulda seen them kids running and hollering from around him like he was Godzilla come to town. He was a wet, scalded, scrawny looking something, water or snot or both runnin out his nose, hands to his side like he in high noon and waiting for the draw. Hollering way cross the hall to the fool with the gun.

"Shoot me. Shoot me, motherfucker. Shoot me. You so bad. Shoot me!"

HILLARY: For real?

JAKE: I know this boy don't really know what he is sayin. He does not truly wish to be shot. Fool with gun is lifting it to aim and fire. I got him by the wrist, and I'm breaking his wrist down with my knee.

HILLARY: Jesus! You coulda been shot.

JAKE: The thought crossed my mind. But I'm disarming this fool and I'm cussing. Call him twenby-leven dumb son'bitches. I am really tough—once I got that gun out of his hand.

HILLARY: Where were the on duty?

JAKE [*shrugs*]: Here come Charlie at last. Looking flushed—my police chaperone, my friend, my partner, he's been busy out in his car with some little girl . . .

HILLARY: Was she eighteen?

JAKE: Barely. Charlie grabs the suicidal fool from the center of the dance floor and I got Machine Gun Kelly and this water, by the way, is steady flowin out the john.

HILLARY: What were they doin in there?

JAKE: Hillary, do you know what the fight was over?

[HILLARY *shakes her head no.*]

Toilet tissue. Somebody used up the last square of toilet tissue.

[*Both laughing.*]

We couldn't stop the water. And the steam rising up—john was like a steam bath. Charlie took two of the boys to the hospital—scalded. I closed down the set. Told all of them young Negroes to get out of my line of vision. I told em "Get the hell out of here you raping, robbing, burglarizing, stick-up artists. Get the f. out of my sight."

HILLARY: You didn't mean that. You love those kids.

JAKE: I meant it at the time. [*Relents*] I can't stand the sight of them for three or four months at least.

HILLARY [*casually*]: What time did you turn them out?

JAKE: Eleven thirty-five. Jam hadn't even started smoking good.

HILLARY: How were the cards tonight?

JAKE: Not bad. Got this light notion—very light—on my right shoulder. Lady Luck looking over my shoulder for a minute. Didn't do bad . . . You know me too well, woman.

HILLARY [*dryly*]: I know you had to have been out of that hall by twelve-thirty. And it's three-thirty by my clock. How much you drop on them cards?

JAKE: Not much.

HILLARY [*inordinately angry*]: A dime is too much.

JAKE [*righteously angry*]: What is this, woman? You act like I have pawned my TV and your TV and best suit to pay gambling debts. I have walked through boiling water this evening. I have faced down nutty undercovers and runny nosed thug with a gun with my bare hands. Hey! I have walked the straight and narrow. If I get any tighter I'll be pigeon-toed. You got microscopes in your eyes; you keep going over me with an electron scope—magnifying faults. I'm okay. I drink a little. I don't get drunk. I lay a light rap here and there. You told me I was free. We ain't traded no wedding bands. And that ain't my fault. Every so often I play poker. I might dream a number and play it. Damn. I like to whisper my name in Ms. Luck's ear, just so she'll remember me every now and then. Just so she'll remember who I am and smile in my lifetime . . . Hillary, sweetheart, you ought to play this hand. I ain't a bad deal.

HILLARY [*moved by his speech, and turning to the stove to prepare his dish*]: Is that another one of your lightweight rap proposals?

JAKE: You don't know when I'm serious. I thought you knew when I was serious.

[*He looks at her back, approaches her gently.*]

Your food even looks good. You could have been an artist.

HILLARY: I could have been a lot of things. That's why I like this stew. Comfort's stew. It could have been a lot of things. Could have been a peanut butter sandwich my—kids—love. It could have been gumbo. Want a taste?

JAKE: I want more than a taste. You don't know that by now?

[*Pulls her close. Playful.*]

I like your crab legs. They got a nice pinch to them.

HILLARY: You know there's no crab legs in here. I couldn't afford them.

JAKE: Your crab legs are meaty and sorta savory.

HILLARY: You talkin pretty unsavory now.

[JAKE *caresses her, buttocks and all.*]

JAKE: You a full bowl of womanhood.

HILLARY: You tryin to signify?

JAKE: I ain't complainin. I welcome the feast.

[*He begins to draw her away from the stove toward the exit stage right. He turns off the stove.*]

HILLARY: Does your mind run on one track?

JAKE: That track is you.

HILLARY [*wants to resist*]: I got an awful lot on my mind, Jacob.

JAKE: Just let me hold you and sing you a lullabye or two. You need to rest.

[*Slow fade as they exit to back.*]

ACT TWO

SCENE 1

HILLARY [*in Memory Space*]: One time when a storm was coming
in and all the other children had gone home early, Enjoli and I
played hide-and-seek. [*Simulates play.*]

Last night, night before
Twenty-four robbers at my door
I got up let em in
Hit em in the head with a rollin pin

All hid?

Better hide good, Jolie, or I'll find out, and you'll be it. Uh-oh . . .
Is that the top of a head where the soft spot used to be I see? . . . Is
that an arm and a leg, precious as can be?

You were never It, Enjoli. I never found you. You came out of
hiding for juice and cookies. "Enjoli, cookies and juice and you're
not It." This evening are you playing hide while we go seek?
Please say yes.

A house-to-house search.

ALFREDA: Knock knock.

HILLARY: I'm looking for Enjoli Rodgers, daughter of Patrice Rodgers. Who is Patrice Rodgers? Your neighbor. She lives two doors from you.

ALFREDA: Knock knock.

HILLARY: I wanna say "Who is it?"

ALFREDA/ENJOLI: Enjoli. En-you-leavin- me lost too long?

The neighbors say nothing

Or the neighbors say a stranger led me away.

The neighbors say I am sure a pretty girl

And smart too.

The neighbors say

They don't know me or my mama or her mama neither.

The neighbors say Who her daddy?

The neighbors say

Leave me alone.

I got to get up and go to work at four-thirty in the morning.

Why don't she know where her own child is?

You spoze to watch em.

HILLARY: Another afternoon I sang to her while she closed her eyes.

HILLARY AND ALFREDA:
Three little children lying in bed,
Two were sick and the other most dead.
Call up the doctor, the doctor said,
Feed them children some shortnin bread.

Oh, Mama's little baby love shortnin shortnin,
Mama's little baby love shortnin bread.
Mama's little baby love shortnin bread.

[HILLARY *moves to the kitchen to cook.*]

HILLARY: Another afternoon her mama came late.

JAKE: Who?

HILLARY: Enjoli's mama.

JAKE: Does she work?

HILLARY: Yeah. She's had a couple of jobs since I've been at the day-care center. Clerk for a while. Now she works at some mail order place. She hates it. She comes to pick up Enjoli when she gets off work. Sometimes she doesn't come straight home.

One day she came to pick her up, she was real late. Came in apologizing and stuff. She was in a hurry. I watched her go into the room where Enjoli was. She didn't know I could see them really. I could just see her. I couldn't see Enjoli where I was. Just Patrice. She was strange to me, because she was so happy that day. Excited . . .

[*Fade to the Memory Space. Lights go up on* PATRICE.]

PATRICE: Ooooh, don't you look so pretty. Mrs. Clay did yo hair? You look so pretty. Come here. I got something for you. Moomy got something for you. I bought you a present. Moomy brought you a present.

HILLARY: The child wouldn't go to her. Children can be ornery. Patrice started to beg her to come to her.

PATRICE [*unwrapping the package and getting down on her knees*]:
See? See what Moomy brought you? A pretty new snowsuit. It's
pink too. The lady in the store say it's cloud pink. You look pretty
in pink. I told her my little girl look so pretty in pink. Come on.
Let me put your snowsuit on you, Enjoli.

Eric say we can go out to get some fried chicken. He takin us to
Kentucky Fried Chicken. Ain't that nice?

And you gone wear yo pretty pink snowsuit.

HILLARY [*remembering a difficult memory*]: I heard a car horn. Long
and insistent. Patrice got real excited then. When the little girl
still didn't come, a change came over Patrice.

PATRICE [*standing*]: Enjoli, bring yo little ass over here. Eric is waitin
for us. You know you don't want Eric to get mad at us . . . Sometimes I just wanta leave you somewhere. You get on my fuckin
nerves.

[*Fade on Memory Space as lights go up in kitchen.*]

JAKE: She cussed at her baby like that?

HILLARY: She had her when she was fourteen.

JAKE: I don't care when she had that little girl.

HILLARY: I was a divorced teen mother so I can feel for her.

JAKE: I feel for the child.

HILLARY: I didn't say that.

JAKE: You implied it.

HILLARY: Okay. You did take care of your sons.

JAKE: Yeah, I do. I washed diapers. Made formula. Take them to school. Check their homework. I keep the music going. How do you keep the music going with the radio turned down so low? Do you hear that? That's our jam.

[JAKE *turns up the radio and sings while he captures her in slow drag.*]

> *You're my love.*
> *You're my angel.*
> *You're the girl of my dreams.*
> *I'd like to thank you for waitin here patiently.*
> *Daddy's home.*
> *Daddy's home to stay—*

[*They dance for a moment. Then* HILLARY *breaks off the dance.*]

HILLARY: Do you know what she said to me one time, Jake, she said, she said—

[*Mimicking* ENJOLI] "Do you know my daddy? I saw him one time but the sun was in my eyes so I couldn't see his face. I don't know what he looks like."

JAKE: Don't matter what he looks like. It's what he does.

[JAKE *starts up dance again.*]

[*The scene goes black. When the lights come up again,* HILLARY *and* JAKE *are dressed for outdoors with flyers in hand.*]

JAKE: We'll blanket the streets. Put these on every lamp post. No one will escape her eyes. [*Simulates reading flyer*] Have you seen her?

[*Enter* SOJOURNER.]

SOJOURNER: Have you seen her? Have you seen her? Who did these?

HILLARY: We worked with her mother. They're good, aren't they?

SOJOURNER [*reading*]: Enjoli Rodgers. Four years old. Thirty pounds. Black hair in cornrows, brown eyes. Last seen in her home, although a witness saw her being led away by a stranger, male six foot two, black hair, beige jacket. Call 773-555-9799. Or bring Enjoli back to her home at 7827 S. Cato . . . Mama, you think they gone bring Enjoli back so they can be accused of stealing her?

HILLARY: They can call the police. Drop her off at a church or firehouse.

SOJOURNER: What's next, milk cartons?

HILLARY: What?

SOJOURNER: Nothing.

HILLARY: What?

SOJOURNER: What's Patrice doing while you're doin all this?

HILLARY: She and Eric are posting flyers in businesses along Seventy-Ninth Street. Her mother is at the house. Patrice is afraid to be gone long from the phone. Can you blame her?

SOJOURNER: I guess not. Give me some. My friends are in the car. We can take Seventy-Fifth.

HILLARY: That's my girl!

[*Exit* SOJOURNER *as* HILLARY *and* JAKE *confer about where to post more flyers. The Chi-Lites' "Have You Seen Her" comes up.*]

SCENE 2

[*Spotlight on* ALFREDA]

ALFREDA: Hillary used to run away every other week. One year she ran away twelve times. She'd pack her bags and go around the corner to her auntie's house. We'd let her spend the night. They'd send her home in the morning. It's fun to run away when you don't have far to go and still be home. Do you feel like rememberin, Hillary? Your feet are sure tired from pounding the cement. Sit down and put yo feet up and rest a while.

[HILLARY *and* SOJOURNER *in the Memory Space.*]

SOJOURNER: Aren't you goin to ask me what I think of him?

HILLARY: Nope. He's my boyfriend.

SOJOURNER: He's not as handsome as my daddy.

HILLARY: Looks may deceive. But in this case he's my kind of fine.

SOJOURNER: He's a head-buster. He's a cop.

HILLARY: Head-buster? He's a detective.

SOJOURNER: He's an absentee father.

HILLARY: What's your daddy? Jake shares custody with his ex.

[*Bumping hips with daughter at stove.* SOJOURNER *peeks at stew.*]

Girl, get out of that pot. Let it heat up good. You got no gift for delayed gratification.

SOJOURNER: I want it all now.

[ALFREDA *eavesdropping, whispers.*]

ALFREDA: You'll live ninety and some, Sojourner. I asked.

HILLARY: Some lives are short as the blink of an eye.

[HILLARY *resting in the present.*]

SOJOURNER: I hate to see you so worried. [*Sounds from the front of the house.*] Somebody's at the door. I'll get it.

[PATRICE *is at the door.*]

HILLARY: Patrice, oh, honey, you're worn out. Come in here. Let me fix you something to eat. I bet you can't remember when you last ate.

PATRICE: I ate a hot dog with Enjoli.

HILLARY: No telling when that was.

SOJOURNER: Patrice, how ya doin?

[PATRICE *does not answer. Another knock at the door.* SOJOURNER *opens it and* JAKE *enters.*]

ALFREDA [*agitated, looking at* PATRICE]: I went to the rock to hide my face. The rocks cried out, "No hiding place. No hiding place down here."

SOJOURNER [*to* JAKE]: What's wrong?

JAKE [*looks at her, trying to remember her name. His gaze lingers on* HILLARY]: Sojourner.

HILLARY: What do you know?

JAKE [*shrugging his left shoulder*]: It's bad, Hillary. They found that little girl.

[JAKE *turns to* PATRICE.]

SOJOURNER: She's alive, isn't she?

PATRICE: Mama.

JAKE [*looking at* PATRICE]: You don't want to know this.

HILLARY: Tell me.

JAKE: Her body was found in an abandoned building.

HILLARY: Tell me.

JAKE: Burns on her hands.

HILLARY: Oh, God!

JAKE: Burns on her back. Her head caved in.

SOJOURNER: Who would do that? Who would do that?

JAKE: The officers on the case say they think she was abducted.
Charlie's working on the case now. He said somebody murdered
her somewhere else and took her there. Afterwards.

SOJOURNER: Did they . . . ?

JAKE: They don't believe she was raped.

SOJOURNER [*outraged*]: But somebody raped her life.

HILLARY, PATRICE, ALFREDA [*doubling over in the same gesture of
grief*]:

Oh, my baby, baby.

PATRICE: Precious Lord!

ALFREDA: God Almighty delivered you to Himself.

HILLARY: Deliver us.

SOJOURNER: Poor little Enjoli!

HILLARY [*concentrating on mundanities*]: Sojourner, turn the fire off from under that stuff in a little while. Will you be here for a while longer?

[HILLARY *leads* PATRICE *to the back.*]

Patrice needs to rest now.

SOJOURNER: I told Mike to pick me up here tomorrow, Mama.

[HILLARY *turns in the door frame and looks at* JAKE. *It is a plaintive, desperate look. Richly controlled.*]

[JAKE *moves toward her, but she exits behind* PATRICE.]

JAKE: I'll be here, Hillary.

[JAKE *paces and talks to* SOJOURNER *as* ALFREDA *listens.*]

I didn't tell her all of it.

SOJOURNER [*whispers*]: More?

JAKE: They talking about taking Patrice in. They think she may have done it to her own child. Child— what was left of her!

SOJOURNER [*furious*]: Those dumb dogs. It's bad enough she finds out her baby's dead. Now they wanna torture her with those kinda accusations.

JAKE: Cruel and inhumane, huh?

SOJOURNER: Yes, and you know it is.

JAKE: Well, I'm cruel and stupid too. Because as God is my witness, I think that girl had a hand in killing her own baby. I think she snapped.

SOJOURNER: No!

[JAKE *moves toward the bedroom.*]

Are you gonna tell Mama?

JAKE: Yeah. Yeah. I'm tellin her.

[*Slow fade as light goes up in the Memory Space.* ALFREDA *sings in the encroaching darkness. It is a rough, simple song. Like Taj Mahal. Or she speaks song.*]

ALFREDA:

Oh, Jesus, won't you come by here.
Oh, Jesus, won't you come by here.
Jesus, won't you come by here.
Now is the needin time
Oh, now is the needin time
Jesus, won't you come by here.

[*Fade to black.*]

ACT 3

SCENE 1

[*It is hours later.* HILLARY *goes to stir the pot in the kitchen.* JAKE *and* SOJOURNER *play separate games of solitaire side-by-side on a table in front of the sofa-bench.*]

SOJOURNER [*watching* JAKE *a little*]: Mama used to play solitaire a lot in the evenings. Or she spent a lot of time with Comfort and her husband. Or reading. But mostly solitaire just after my bedtime. I'd sneak up for some water and Mama would be in the kitchen playing solitaire and cooking tomorrow's dinner. So she could just heat it up when she got home the next day. Or when I was bigger I'd heat it up. Beans or oxtail soup or whatever and make some cornbread. Mama likes cornbread with just about every meal. Did you know that?

JAKE: She's making it now.

SOJOURNER: She got that African stew on the stove again. Do you know Comfort?

JAKE: Not lately.

SOJOURNER: Not that comfort. I'm talking about the Ghanaian woman named Comfort who used to live downstairs. What was I talking about?

JAKE: I don't know.

SOJOURNER: As long as you and Mama been going together, you know this is the first extended conversation we have ever had. I never had much to say to Mama's boyfriends.

[*He's listening now, but trying to act the same.*]

You ever meet my daddy?

JAKE: Naw. He anything like you?

SOJOURNER: Not really. I get more like my mother every day . . . but she used to say I was just like him. I knew how to get my way. So charming and all.

JAKE: Got a good opinion of yourself too.

SOJOURNER: I got that from my mother . . . I was asking you about my daddy because you and he are nothing alike.

JAKE: We don't remind you of each other. You noticed that.

SOJOURNER: As a matter of fact, you not like any of Mama's boyfriends.

JAKE: All told, how many has she had?

[SOJOURNER *instructs him to move a card. Then moves one of her own.*]

SOJOURNER: Not many. When you're a single mother with a daughter you got to be careful around these no good men. That's what my mama's friend Comfort says and she's been married to Mr. Smith for twenty-three years. My grandmother used to say these low-down men.

JAKE: Hillary told me about her ex-friend Albert.

SOJOURNER: Albert the Groper? Mr. Macon. Yeah. When I was a little girl he used to have me reach into his pants' pocket for change all the time. It was his big thrill. I didn't know it. My mama didn't either. Cause I didn't tell her how he kept me stocked with Hershey's with almonds and Nestlé Crunches. If I had known how the Nestlé corporation operated in the Third World, exploiting poor mothers into using muddy water formula instead of their own breast milk, I would never have kept up that chocolate habit. Well, he was getting his thrills every day for about six months, till I had ten cavities in my mouth. I had kinda moved on to potato chips with hot sauce by then.

JAKE [*laughing at her story and her*]: Girl, you oughtta quit.

SOJOURNER: One day when I was ten, Mama caught him with a mouth-drooped-open, slack-jawed drool on his face and lust clouds in his eyes looking at me in my sundress. Mama told him to get out. He kept asking her with this simply idiotic grin on his face, "What I do, Hillary?" "What I do?" Mama said, "It's not what you did, it's what you were thinking about doing." She had too much class for him anyway. My mama is an aristocrat. Ain't too many men around for aristocrats. That's why I'm going to marry Mike while he's in law school and we can grow old together.

JAKE: I guess I should be glad that you're grown. It's okay for me to come around now.

[JAKE *throws down his cards. Gets his coat. Calls to* HILLARY.]

Anything I can get you, darlin?

HILLARY: No. Nothing.

JAKE: Pretend. Act like you need me.

HILLARY: I do need you. More than I can say.

[*They gaze at each other with understanding.*]

JAKE: Going to the station house. See what I can find out. Bye, baby.

[*Exit* JAKE.]

ALFREDA: The neighbors say

What kinda trouble we in?

Who commit this sin?

The neighbors say

Whoever did it

Took a life before it had a life.

Whoever did it—stranger—or relative

Is going to pay.

Has got to pay.

The neighbors say

They may run

But they can't really hide.

If they hide, we'll seek them out.

The neighbors say

We'll hunt em down and hang em from the highest tree.

The neighbors say

Whoever did it is history.

Like she is.

SCENE 2

[*Next day in the kitchen, midday.*]

HILLARY: I thought you and Sojourner liked solitaire.

JAKE: We're playing spades.

SOJOURNER: Spades, Mama. You wanna play?

HILLARY: Sojourner, didn't I ask you to make some rice?

SOJOURNER: There's some left.

HILLARY: I want brown rice.

SOJOURNER: I'll have to go get it.

JAKE: The bread is fine, Hillary.

HILLARY: Sojourner, do what your mother told you.

SOJOURNER: Don't look at my cards.

[*Exit* SOJOURNER.]

HILLARY: How'd your kids like the movie?

JAKE: Are you kiddin? They loved it. I slept through half of it.

HILLARY: Some company you are. Are you giving them enough time?

JAKE: It's quality time. They get all of me when I'm with them. We talked over pizza.

HILLARY: Jake, maybe we shouldn't see each other so much.

JAKE: Woman, what are you talkin about?

HILLARY: Maybe you should spend more time with your boys.

JAKE: And less with your girl?

ALFREDA: And less with your girl.

HILLARY: You're twistin things all around.

ALFREDA: You're twistin things all around. Be careful, daughter.

JAKE: What's my name, Hillary?

HILLARY: Jake.

JAKE: No. What's my name?

HILLARY: Jacob Theodore Sunnyside.

JAKE: Well then. And Sojourner is Sojourner. Not Enjoli.

HILLARY: She could be, Jake.

JAKE: Any of us could be dead. Chicago is a cold city. I'm a cop, remember. A real cop. We're going to find who did it. Can I take a break and spend time with my kids and play cards with your child ?

HILLARY: Don't let the trail get cold, Jacob. They think Patrice did it.

JAKE: Who's the police, me or you? You been watching "Hill Street Blues" or "Dragnet" reruns. It's not my case, but I guess I can get some information. They're getting tired of me pestering them. When a man loves a woman. The things I do for you.

[*Light on* ALFREDA.]

ALFREDA: Comes a shadow time of sorrow and grief beyond grief. The ancestors say "Hold tight to each other." There's a bad storm coming. Comes a shadow time of sorrow and grief beyond grief.

[*Lights dim.*]

SCENE 3

[*Hours later. Enter* JAKE.]

JAKE: Nothing new.

HILLARY: Nothing?

JAKE: Nothing.

HILLARY: Thank you. I'm glad I met your mother.

JAKE: Not her son.

HILLARY: Do I have to say that? You never met my mother. I can still feel the way she used to hug me. Real tight. No devils could get through that embrace.

JAKE: We won't let any devils in here either.

HILLARY: I keep thinking about my mother. Her and Enjoli.

JAKE: Where'd Sojourner go?

HILLARY: She went to the store again. Probably stopped over at a friend's house. She just wanted to get out of here. I don't blame her.

JAKE: Kinda late for her to be out alone.

HILLARY: Mother-hen. Sojourner knows to get a ride home if she needs one.

[*Soft knocking at the door.*]

That's her now. Forgot her key.

JAKE: I got it.

[JAKE *opens the front door.* PATRICE *is there. Caught up in the wind. In jeans and a short leather jacket. Little kerchief over badly permed hair.*]

PATRICE [*timidly*]: Mr. Clay.

JAKE: Sunnyside. Jacob Sunnyside. What can I do for you? Mrs. Clay is busy right now.

PATRICE [*talking more to herself than to* JAKE.]: Oh. She's busy.

[PATRICE *turns to leave.*]

Just tell her Patrice Rodgers stopped by to see her.

JAKE [*grabbing her by the elbow*]: Hey, wait a minute. Don't go. Hillary, Patrice Rodgers is here.

HILLARY: Let her in, Jake.

JAKE: Come in, Patrice. Let me take your coat.

[PATRICE *gives him her jacket.*]

[*Enter* SOJOURNER *in doorway.*]

SOJOURNER [*to* PATRICE]: I'm sorry—for your loss.

PATRICE: I remember you. You go to college. Don't you? You real smart.

SOJOURNER [*embarrassed*]: Yeah. I go to college.

PATRICE [*can't take her eyes from* SOJOURNER]: I never liked school. Except for math. I could do numbers good. But I just didn't like school. None of them teachers. Enjoli, she like you. She love school. She love Mrs. Clay. She like Mrs. Clay daughter.

[SOJOURNER *looks at* HILLARY *nervously.* HILLARY *gives* SOJOURNER *a reassuring sign by touching* PATRICE's *shoulder.* SOJOURNER *takes off her coat and hangs it on the coatrack. She and* JAKE *share a puzzled glance.* JAKE *is sitting now.* SOJOURNER *leans on the windowsill next to* JAKE. HILLARY *grips* SOJOURNER's *shoulder.*]

PATRICE [*eyes still on* SOJOURNER]: Maybe Enjoli go to college. She love, she loves to go to school . . . She loves the way you teach them at the school. All she talk about in the evening is Mrs. Clay. Mrs. Clay this. Mrs. Clay that. Every time you comb her hair she won't let me touch it for a week. She say she a princess in her cornrows. She don't want to go to sleep or she might mess up her hair.

[*She speaks in a child's voice.*]

"Mrs. Clay showed we how to fix salad. Mrs. Clay showed we how to plant some seeds. Mrs. Clay let we make Easter baskets. Christmas trees." I buy her all kinds of toys but she just play with that black Raggedy Ann doll Mrs. Clay made her.

[*A red spotlight begins to train on* PATRICE, *while the living room and kitchen area goes dim.*]

"Mrs. Clay made we Halloween masks. We made pictures of Reverent Doctor Martha Lutha King, Malcolm X, Fannie Lou Hamer, and Rosa Parks. I can say my alphabets. Listen, Moomie. I know my numbers." And I listen at her numbers. I was good at numbers in school. I listen and Eric listen too. She say, "Eric, listen at my numbers."

[PATRICE *has eyes fixed on* SOJOURNER. SOJOURNER *is* ENJOLI *to her.* HILLARY *wants to stop her, but* JAKE *signals no.*]

"My name is Enjoli Rodgers. I am almost four years old. I am a big girl."

JAKE: A neighbor said she saw Enjoli with a stranger. Do you know who that stranger might be?

PATRICE: I don't know. I don't know who a stranger might be. Maybe it was Enjoli's daddy.

JAKE: What's his name?

PATRICE: The police talked to him. He was in jail for parking tickets. A stranger? Do you think a stranger got my baby?

JAKE: Do you?

HILLARY: Stop it, Jake.

PATRICE: It happened in Atlanta. They came up in the house and took that little girl.

JAKE: Atlanta.

PATRICE: Uh huh. That's what Eric said.

JAKE: Eric knows a lot.

PATRICE: Eric is real smart. He took two years of college.

JAKE: Bright boy.

PATRICE: He doesn't like 'boy.' He got mad when I said "Boy, you so crazy."

JAKE: Is he?

PATRICE: What?!

HILLARY: Jacob, let her rest.

JAKE: Crazy.

PATRICE: No. I was just sayin.

JAKE [*rapid fire*]: Why'd you kill your own baby, Patrice?

PATRICE: I didn't!

HILLARY: Man, have you lost your mind?

JAKE: You're gonna burn in hell, Patrice.

HILLARY: No.

JAKE: You're gonna burn in hell.

HILLARY: This has got to stop.

JAKE: Your fingerprints were all over that little girl.

PATRICE: No!

JAKE: You killed your own baby and put her body in a box and hid it in a dumpster like garbage. What kind of a mother are you?

HILLARY: She's the mother who worked and kept her child well-fed, clean, and dressed nice. Doin the best she could. Why you blamin this child? Would you do that to Sojourner?

JAKE: She's not you, Hillary.

HILLARY: Oh, yes, she is. Fingerprints on a body—whoever? Jake, let her rest.

JAKE: No. No. Hell, no.

HILLARY: Always. Always. Who's to blame? These teen-aged mothers chewin their gum. Talkin loud on the back of the bus, a baby at her breast and another one on her lap. Whose fault is it when baby makes three? Not the boy who didn't wear a condom, but the girl who didn't take the pill. Mama's baby; papa's maybe. These babies having babies, if they weren't babies they'd be more responsible, but it's the girl's fault. She has to be born responsible. Who's to blame for these high taxes but these teenage welfare mothers eatin up the economy. Black teenage mothers. Who's gonna take the blame for a shameful infant mortality rate? Who's gonna take the blame? Put it on her. Slap. Slap. Be quiet. I tole you to be quiet. Who's gonna take the blame? Put it on her. Run out to the store for five minutes. Padlock the burglar gate, leave the babies alone, lock them in, lock out the harm. Fire! Five minutes. Everything's gone. Babies. Who's gonna take the blame? Put it on her. All these baby-madonnas we have to cherish them so they can cherish their babies. We have to cherish them and their babies.

[*To* PATRICE.]

There's no hiding place, Patrice. No hiding place. Just tell the truth. The truth is the only light. It will make you whole. Tell it and they'll leave you alone.

PATRICE [*remembering, under a red spotlight*]: She kept buggin me about goin to school. She cried because she wasn't going to school. I told her to be quiet because Eric was tryin to sleep, but she kept on cryin to go to school. And he got up and he come in the room and he tell her to shut up and she act like she scared of him so she scream and he ball up his fist and he shook his fist at her and I was ironing and he just snatch up the iron and he say, "I'll fix you. I'll fix you. Feel the heat." He was just teasin her you know and I said uh—uhnnnnnn, Eric, but before the words were out my mouth she kinda stumbled forward and the iron got her on her hands. And she screamed, but no sound was comin out her mouth. But her eyes was wide open and then she was screamin in her eyes jacked open. And he said, "Look what you done, stupid." And he started shakn her shakin her to make her be quiet. Shakin. Shakin and pushed her. And he pushed her real hard away from the iron and she fell back on the radiator and her

48

head scrunched up against the radiator and steam was comin out on her and she was tangled up on the floor and I said, "Eric, look what you done did!"

And he said, "I didn't mean to . . . I was just scarin her. You saw. You saw it." She . . . her body went all everywhicha way when I picked her up and I said, "I got to take her, take her to the hospital," and he said, "Hide her. Hide her. Help me hide her. I'll go to jail, baby. Help me, mama, help me." So I helped him. I put on her snowsuit. Her pink snowsuit. And I zipped it up. Eric wiped up the blood around the radiator. He washed it and washed and wrenched it ten times over and over. Look like it was real cold outside. The wind was blowin so hard. Enjoli was all cold. I wanted to go back inside, but Eric say, "Come on. We gotta go." We slipped out the backdoor and snuck down the alley and up aways to that big ole abandoned building and we climed up through the wine and whiskey bottles and the pee, and the broken-down stuff that people threw out they house or left there and Eric stuffed her body down in the dump. He punched it and pushed it down in the dump good and he told me "Let's go." "Let's go. Leave her here." And I said, "I can't leave her here. She might get cold." But she was cold. "It's cold in that place and it's so dirty." He told me, "Come on or I'll leave you in there with her." Then he pushed me out. But he didn't mean that either. Eric didn't mean that. He just wanted to get me away from there so that he wouldn't go to jail. I don't want Eric to go to jail.

She looked so pretty in her pink snowsuit.

ALFREDA/ENJOLI:

The neighbors say

Come to think of it

I heard a scream.

I heard a baby cryin

And cryin

Then I heard a scream.

The neighbors say

I knew he did it.

The neighbors say

Come to think of it

I heard a scream

From someone small.

The neighbors say

They knew the boyfriend killed me

With his bare hands.

The neighbors say

That mama didn't have good sense.

The neighbors say

These teen mothers.

The neighbors say

It's a sin and a shame.

The neighbors say

Enjoli. She's a perfume.

We can smell her everywhere.

On the news. In our hearts.

A sweet perfume.

I bring tears to your eyes.

[*Lights go up as* SOJOURNER *rushes to the bedroom with her hand over her mouth.* JAKE *has moved toward the phone; by the time the lights encompass all, he is talking on the phone.* HILLARY *sits transfixed. She and* PATRICE *are frozen, looking into each other's eyes.*]

JAKE: Charlie, yeah, me. Could you come over in your car. Patrice Rodgers is here—over Hillary's—and she got something to tell you.

[*He turns to look at the girl.*]

Yeah. Something like that.

HILLARY: Patrice, do you know what you just said?

PATRICE: Huh? I got to write down the address. She waiting for you in her pretty pink snowsuit. I didn't comb her hair. She like when you do it. She want to go to school. She real smart.

HILLARY: Patrice, where is Eric now?

PATRICE: The police let him go. He went away. I don't know where he is. He got to come back for me. He not going to leave me now. Is he? I shoulda let her come here. She just make trouble between me and him.

HILLARY: Where is Enjoli's father?

PATRICE: He don't claim her. Eric not her daddy. She just keep on making trouble between me and him. Mama want her to come live in the whiskey bottle with her. But I shoulda brought her here. Your man, he wouldn't mind her, would he?

[JAKE *stands next to* PATRICE. *Takes her by the elbow.*]

JAKE: Patrice, Mrs. Clay is tired now. She has to get some rest. Some friends of mine want to talk to you. I'll go with you.

HILLARY: I'm coming too. She—needs somebody.

[*Fade.*]

SCENE 4

[*Takes place in the Memory Space. The funeral parlor.* HILLARY *is in a white suit. The space is empty.* HILLARY *is in a blue light.*]

HILLARY: Yes. No. Mrs. Rodgers asked me to see after her. Yes. It is. So sad. She was a beautiful child. I couldn't help but love her. Could we be alone for a little while? I promised her grandmother I'd comb her hair and see to her.

[HILLARY *approaches the imaginary casket.*]

Oh, you! There you are. Here. Let me. I'm just going to make two big cornrows one on each side. Part it in the center.

[*Bends down, begins to braid. Her braiding and caressing the body is a dance, ancient, maternal, exquisitely anguished.*]

Oh, aren't you pretty, little one. So pretty. No mark on you where he smashed . . .

[*More conversational.*]

When I was coming out the door, found it on the floor. Who left it? A postcard photograph by James Van Der Zee, a Black photographer. It was sad, but too sweet. A baby in a casket with angels sitting around watching over her. Do you see them? . . . I want you to open your eyes and look at me, Enjoli.

[*She waits.*]

No miracles today. You ain't here. Someplace wiser. I want to believe that in your tiny time here you know more than I do now. Why? Why he killed you. Why she didn't protect you. Why she helped him hide you. You know, there's no hiding place. Not down here.

[*Stares into invisible coffin. Reaches into her pocket.*]

I brought your puppet. Let me tuck it under your hand. Oh, the burns don't show anymore.

[*Begins to croon.*]

Mama's little baby / loves shortnin / shortnin. Mama's little baby loves shortnin bread . . .

[*Doesn't finish. Listens to an unheard question.*]

Yes. I'm finished. Thank you for letting us be alone.

[*Fade.*]

SCENE 5

[HILLARY's *kitchen, a few hours after the funeral.*]

JAKE: That girl was probably more upset that her boyfriend's in jail than her baby's in the ground.

HILLARY: At least Mrs. Rodgers got up the money to get her out for the funeral.

JAKE: Did you help her?

[HILLARY *doesn't answer.*]

SOJOURNER [*coming out with luggage in hand*]: Comfort called to see how you were doing, but she said don't bother to call her back. She'll be talking to you later.

[HILLARY *opens her arms for her daughter.*]

HILLARY: Thanks for staying overtime with your mama, sweetie pie.

SOJOURNER: You my baby.

HILLARY: Oh, I'm the mama alright.

[*They embrace as* JAKE *collects* SOJOURNER's *luggage, takes it to the car.*]

   Don't you get behind in your studies.

SOJOURNER: Please, Mama, I am the kid, remember. Your daughter.

[*Another hug.*]

   Take care of my mama, Mister Police.

JAKE: Is that an order or what?

SOJOURNER: That's The Law.

JAKE: I must uphold it.

[*He salutes* SOJOURNER. *She salutes him.*]

ALFREDA: I like this part. I like the way things are turning out.

[*Car horn.*]

SOJOURNER: That's Mike's horn. You two be good now.

HILLARY: You turning into a regular mama.

SOJOURNER: Yeah.

[*Not smiling. Looks them both full in the face. She's very serious.*]

Good-bye. I miss you both already.

[SOJOURNER *exits. Closes the door.*]

[HILLARY *notices flowers on the table. Reads note to* JAKE.]

HILLARY: Dear Mama, Keep your sunnyside up. Please send me recipe for wonderful dish you've made that nourishes me and spices up my life. Thank you. Sojourner Truth Clay.

JAKE: Sunnyside up. That's me. Even in tough times. You got a lot going on in you now and I'm here.

HILLARY [*moving briskly in the kitchen and talking conversationally*]: I know you are.

I like plenty of vegetables in my African stew. Greenery and things full of vitamins and juices. That's not the way Comfort showed me exactly. It ain't her recipe. What kinda cook would I be if I followed somebody else's recipe to the letter without makin it my own?

JAKE: What kind of woman would you be?

[*They look at each other and smile.*]

[*She's talking to him now.*]

HILLARY: It's a delicious dish, seafood, okra, good and loose like the beginning of life. I may omit peanut butter for my daughter's sake. The aroma of it floods my kitchen and I guess my neighbors can smell it now. Can smell my good life assailing them aromatically. I keep going back for seconds. This is the dish of life.

[*Hands* JAKE *a dish.*]

I loved a child who tasted it once. And I think I feel her here now with me, with us, and she is a mothering angel sliding through the cells of this moment.

[HILLARY *places a dish and a glass in the window for the ancestors,* ALFREDA *and* ENJOLI.]

ALFREDA: She can't tell you the spirit of the cook. The tenderness and generosity. Integrity and compassion. Strength and perseverance. She can't tell you it took a village to raise her and Jake and Sojourner. We have to be strong to raise our strength. We have to remember to dream of yet to be. We have to cherish our own.

HILLARY: I am going back for seconds.

[*She lifts a bowl of African stew. At the same time* JAKE *lifts his bowl.*]

JAKE: I'm going back for seconds.

HILLARY: This is the dish of life and I'm sharing it with my own. Family. Hillary Robinson Clay soon to be Sunnyside is going back for seconds. We're going back for seconds.

[*She strolls toward the back as* JAKE *opens the door for her. He goes back into the kitchen and turns on the radio. Then he follows* HILLARY. *Music floods the stage.*]

ALFREDA [*singing*]:
> There's a sweet sweet spirit
> In this place
> And I know that it's the spirit
> Of the Lord.
>
> There's a joyful expression
> On your face
> And I know that it's the
> Presence of the Lord.
>
> Sweet holy spirit
> Sweet heavenly dove
> Stay right here with us
> Filling us with your love.
>
> And for these blessings
> We lift our hearts in praise
> Without a doubt we know
> We will have been revived
> When we shall leave this place.

[*Fade to black.*]